IDOL WORSHIP

GABRIEL MILLER

Idol Worship

Published by All Peoples Ministries
P.O. Box 30341
Lynchburg, Virginia 24503
www.allpeoplesministries.org

Cover design by Samuel Petty

ISBN-13: 978-0-9987608-2-7
ISBN-10: 0-9987608-2-X

Printed in the United States of America

To Mom, who diligently obeys 1 John 5:21

CONTENTS

INTRODUCTION

My family and I had been living in our new hometown about six months. Now, on a Sunday afternoon, we had just walked out of the 21st church we had visited in that timespan. A nice-sized church, maybe as many as 800 in attendance. Childcare provided. Contemporary music, well-executed. Hands raised. Jesus exalted in the lyrics. Sermon on Joshua 1:8, meditate on the Word day and night. Scriptural, well-delivered, good application. Friendly people, on the way in and on the way out, as far as I recall.

We got our two boys buckled into the back of our Explorer, and away we drove. We made it two blocks. I pulled over, shifted into park, and began to weep.

"How is that good enough?" I managed to spit out. "All of those people are content with that experience. How? When Billy Graham preached, the whole arena came under conviction. Thousands of people would respond to the Spirit. How can people settle for this? You look at those people's faces and there's just nothing there. No hunger. They're not looking for anything more. It's nowhere near their radar."

* * * * *

These are not bad people. I'm not even suggesting they're not believers. But the American church today is full of them. They have slipped from their initial conversion experience into a mere routine. The idea of fervently burrowing directly into the heart of God is foreign to them. This routine, this contentment with the ordinary, this acceptance of a life that is not "filled with all the fullness of God" as Paul writes in Ephesians 3, is symptomatic of an issue in the heart. That issue is *idol worship*.

When we think of idol worship we probably think of Aaron and the golden calf, the prophets of Baal, and the Asherah poles in the high places. Definitely idol worship, and taken to its most disgusting levels. But idol worship does not have to be that extreme. Idol worship can be *just-barely* idol worship. One does not have to reject God totally to be idolatrous; idol worship merely means that God is not first place.

The word *worship*, which comes from the Old English *weorthscipe*, means *to ascribe worth*. In this broad sense of the word, we can and do worship a lot of things. That's why we lock our doors when we go out. If we did not ascribe any worth to the items in our house, there would be no need to lock our doors. Worshipping, or ascribing worth to things, only becomes a problem when we ascribe more worth to the thing than we do to God. This is when we cross the line into idol worship.

With such a low threshold over which to step into idolatry, I think if we're honest with ourselves, we all engage in idol worship from time to time. We do not think "high thoughts" of God, as A.W. Tozer puts it,[1] and from our wrong thinking about God grow wrong behaviors. If these

2

wrong behaviors are not put in check, they grow to become wrong behavior-patterns. This is where I believe much of the American church lies today. Low thoughts of God, wrong behavior-patterns. It's a congregation problem, it's a pastor problem, it's a worship-leader problem, it's a music-industry problem.

This book is a call to the church to take note of our idols, and dispense with them. For the most part, the idols I will deal with in this book are not so much the general idols of life as much as the specific idols of Sunday morning. Most of the people sitting in our churches today assume they are worshipping God-alone, when they're actually worshipping God-and. God and their idols. Their worship of God is only partial, and is therefore unacceptable. Meanwhile their idols are distracting them and preventing them from true and acceptable worship, and they don't even realize it. When we gather for "worship," what are the idols that keep us from actually worshipping God? That is the question answered in this book.

Written to the church in general, certain chapters or sections are particularly directed toward worship leaders and pastors. It is a call to examine what we are doing in our churches and why we are doing it. To pause for a time of introspection, and to call out to the Lord to reveal the things in our hearts that He still desires to root out. I trust that as you make your way through this book, you too will be stirred to repent of the worship of whatever idols you are still holding onto.

You Still Lack One Thing

The rich young ruler was able to list many areas where he was in compliance with the law. But Jesus responded, "You still lack one thing" (Luk 18:22). The fact that *greed* was the *one thing* he needed to repent of is not at all the point of the story. That just happened to be his one thing. The point is that God requires total surrender. We all have one thing. Most of us have more than one thing. But as we learn to surrender more and more, we get to the place where the Lord asks for that one last thing. When we come to that place, we realize what our greatest idol is. So what one thing do you lack?

From Preferences to Idols

We all have preferences. There's nothing wrong with that. The problem is when our preferences become idols. My challenge to you is this: as you read this book, when you come across a chapter that you identify with as a preference, ask yourself whether your preference is actually an idol. And here's how you'll know (I got this one from Bud Crawford, founding pastor of All Peoples Church): *How would you respond if God asked you to give up that preference? Or how would you respond if your pastor or other trusted spiritual authority asked you to give up that preference?* Would you become indignant and resist? Would you push back with everything in you? Would you just find a new church? If so, then that thing is not a preference, it's an idol. If you can't lay down your preference of self, if you can't lay down your preference of entertainment, if you can't lay down your preference of style, if you can't lay down your preference of structure, if you can't lay down your preference of spontaneity, if you can't lay down your preference of emotionalism, if you can't lay down your preference of production, if you can't lay down your preference of tradition, if you can't lay down your preference of freedom, if you can't lay down your preference of musicianship, if you can't lay down your preference of doctrine, if you can't lay down your preference of relevance, if you can't lay down your preference of community, if you can't lay down your preference of ministry; then your preference is not a preference, it's an idol. And it's time to slay it. So, let's get to it!

1
THE IDOL OF SELF

I just got back from the dump. It wasn't really something I wanted to do. But we had a lot of trash piled up in the shed, the kind the regular garbage guys won't pick up—old carpet, large wood and metal scraps, and so forth. And my wife had put that on my honey-do list for this Christmas break. As I started out the door, I told her "I love you," I gave her a hug and a kiss, and then I went out and did what she asked. Let me say that another way: I first *declared* my love to her, then I *expressed* my love to her, then I *demonstrated* my love to her. Declaration, expression, and demonstration are the three ways we reveal the *worth* of an individual or thing. When we ascribe worth to someone or something we are giving *worth-ship*, or, *worship* to that individual or thing. Now, I'm not saying it's ok to worship my wife in the same way I worship God, but it is appropriate for me to ascribe worth to her, to declare, express, and demonstrate to her that she is valuable to me. And of course, it is also right that I worship God in this way: to declare, express, and demonstrate to Him that He is valuable to me. The difference, clearly, is that I must be sure that I ascribe THE MOST worth to God. That I declare, express, and demonstrate to Him that He is worth more to me than is anyone or anything else. If I don't do that, if I show by what I say and do that there are people or things in my life that are worth more to me than God is, then I have descended into idol worship. But if I declare, express, and demonstrate to God that He is worth more to me than is anyone or anything else, then I am truly worshipping. *Worship is declaring, expressing, and demonstrating to God, in reverence and servitude, that He is worth more to me than is anyone or anything else.*

The church today has a much more anemic view of worship than this. For one thing, worship has become synonymous with music—which should not be—and the worship practices associated with this musical experience basically amount to mere *declaration*, and in some churches, *expression*. But when singing time ends and the offering is collected, only 1 in 20 people are willing to *demonstrate* their God is worthy by giving Him 10% of their income. When the church is asked to come back for prayer meeting Tuesday night, only 1 in 5 return to *demonstrate* their God is worthy of their time and relational investment through prayer. When the homeless man stands on the corner with his cardboard sign, few *demonstrate* their God is worthy by helping "the least of these." When the waitress is rude (or maybe even when she's nice) almost no one *demonstrates* that God is worthy by returning a smile, an understanding glance, or an extravagant tip. We have pastors who are more concerned with sermon preparation than with meeting the daily needs of the sheep. We have worship leaders who put in 40 hours a week perfecting a 30-minute musical experience, but have no prayer life and no concept of commitment to service. And we have parishioners who barely give any thought to the things of God outside their Sunday-morning routine. We are simply not *demonstrating* that God is worth-y.

Many in the church today have terminated their worship at the stage of declaration or expression. They do not see acts of service throughout the week as a continuation, through demonstration, of the Sunday-worship event. But all three stages are essential to living a life of true worship. We can declare, but without expression, declaration is cold. We can express, but without demonstration, expression is hollow. A mature believer cannot *declare* God is worthy, yet allow pride to keep him from stepping out into a Spirit-led free *expression* of worship. A mature believer cannot *express* God is worthy, yet allow pride to keep her from walking out that expression through a *demonstration* of service. When we pay lip-service to the preeminence of God, all the while ultimately doing our own thing, we are guilty of worshipping *the idol of self.*

Worship is Serving

The first sin was pride. Satan, thinking himself to be greater than he actually was, attempted to exalt himself above God. And really, all sin originates in pride, because sin is anything that contradicts the nature of God; when we engage in sin we are choosing our own way over God's way, the ultimate act of pride.

In diametric opposition to pride, God calls us to be worshippers. Why do I say worship is the opposite of pride? Because worship, among other things, is serving. The Hebrew and Greek words, *abad* and *latreuo/latreia* respectively, that are translated *worship*, mean *to serve* or *service*. So, for example, when Paul beseeches us by the mercies of God, in Romans 12:1, to present our bodies a living sacrifice, holy and acceptable to God, he calls this act *worship* (ESV, NIV, CSB), or *service* (KJV, NKJV, NET). When we worship God by serving Him and others, we are regarding one another as more important than ourselves (Phl 2:3). In other words we are loving God with all our heart, mind, soul, and strength, and loving our neighbor as ourselves. Only when we do this are we overcoming pride and the idol of self.

I preach service: *service is worship; you're not worshipping if you're not serving.* Well lately I've had the opportunity to walk this out. I've been learning how to serve. I preached it, now God is giving me the opportunity to walk it out. And for the most part, that's not fun. But I thank God for putting me in that position, because now when I preach service, I have some life experience that supports the message.

Many people are just not getting this. In the church today we see too many messages that are not being walked out. We have people who believe they are doing one thing, believe their life is about one thing, believe their purpose and direction is toward one thing, and yet they are really doing their own, alternative thing. There's no explanation other than we are witnessing widespread deception.

No message is being walked out less than the message, "It's all about Him." We say "it's all about Him," and then immediately turn around and reveal to everyone by our actions that on the inside, we really still believe it's all about us. All of our time and resources are devoted to us. When we think, we think about ourselves. When we talk, we talk about ourselves. When we pray, we pray for ourselves. We give work higher priority than family. Or we give family higher priority than God. We choose Little League instead of church. We choose watching the big game instead of checking up on the little widow. We choose to eat out that extra meal instead of feeding many hungry mouths.

Worship leaders love to say "it's all about Him." How many, when we really boil it all down, are only on the platform just to satisfy the carnal desire to be seen? And they don't even realize it.

A couple of winters ago, we had a big snow on a Saturday. We went through the checklist of items to try to make sure we could safely hold a meeting on Sunday. We had a plow guy come and plow the parking lot with his truck. If you don't know anything about snow, a plowing truck leaves remnants that someone has to come along and clean up with a shovel. I volunteered for this job. I drove to the church with a snow shovel and a bag of salt. (Now, I should give a caveat at this point that, as a Florida boy, snow is still a novelty to me, and I actually enjoy doing this kind of work! Be that as it may,) I shoveled off all the walkways and began to scatter salt over the various patches of ice. There, alone in the darkness in sub-freezing temperatures, I teared up as I heard the Lord say "This is Worship!" And I knew that what I was doing at that moment was as important as anything I would do the next morning during "music time."

Worship leader, hear this: *worship is serving*. If we polled your church and asked the people to list the 10 people who they considered to be the Top 10 Servants in the church, where would you rank? Worship leader, I don't care what your title is, and I don't care what you do on Sunday mornings, if your name is not on that list, you are NOT the worship leader of your church.

It is time to stop deluding ourselves into thinking we are worshipping God if we are not willing to prove our worship through demonstrated service.

> By this all will know that you are My disciples,
> if you have love for one another.
>
> –John 13:35

That word *love* means *preferential treatment* or *preferring others to self*. In the words of Bob Dylan, "you're gonna have to serve somebody."

The Need to Self-promote

One way the idol of self manifests is in advertising. What are our real motivations for advertising our churches? And how do we advertise them? I'm not necessarily against advertising outright. I just wonder if, most of the time, advertising is not birthed out of the idol of self that says that "my church" is really what's important, even more important than my God.

Ask the question, "Why are we advertising our church?" Is it because you desire to see people's lives changed by encountering the presence of God? I would imagine many would honestly be able to answer *yes* to this. Some, though, would not. Leaders want to see new people because they equate numbers with successful ministry, or worse, when they see new people they see more income. Church members want to see new people because it enhances their social-club experience.

Let's honestly answer another question: "What kind of people are we hoping to attract?" Sometimes we can answer this by looking at the advertisement itself. Do the images you put forward with your ad subtly say *we're white people looking for more white people*, or *we're middle class people looking for more middle class people*? Does the unspoken message of your image say *church for us is a social outlet*, or does it say *we desire to encounter the living Lord*? I'll just give you a for-instance, if the advertise

11

ment for your church includes a picture of a coffee mug, just rethink it one more time.

If your church is not hoping to attract the destitute, the impoverished and the broken, it probably won't. But what does happen when these folks come in? Are they treated differently? Are we hoping to attract people who can make the church look better, and turning away the very people who need God the most?

Perhaps you were able to answer the first question successfully. You really do desire to see new people come so they can encounter the presence of God. Now it's possible that the problem is that you lack the trust to believe God to send those people without your help? Ladies and gentlemen, much of what we desire to see in terms of church growth can be accomplished in the prayer closet much more efficiently than on the billboard. We can ask God and trust God to bring to our churches those men and women that He desires should be there.

Lyrics

Another way the idol of self can manifest is in our lyrics. Are we singing more about ourselves or about our God? There is a time and a place for man-centered lyrics. There is a time for receiving, there is a time for healing, there is a time for intimacy, there is a time for laughing, there is a time for dancing, there is a time for supplication, and there is a time for getting help. But that time is not all the time. We must make sure that our lyrics declare to the Lord that He is worth more to us than is anyone or anything else. If we are not ascribing worth to Him, we are not really worshipping.

In my grandparents' generation (and in my grandparents' tradition, which is to say, Southern Gospel) they sang song after song about "flying away" and "walking on streets of gold" and disproportionately fewer songs about how God made a way for us to get there. Now I've got no problem getting excited about eternal life in heaven, but if I don't take time to reflect on the cross of Christ that got me there, I'm really missing something.

When I was growing up, the church-world in general was making the transition out of the traditional hymnal and into what was called *praise and worship music*. And there was a lot of good music to come out of that 80's-90's era. But we lost some theological depth in the process. I'm sorry to say that it wasn't until I was 39 years old that I ever sang this weighty text by Augustus Toplady in a church service:

> Rock of Ages, cleft for me,
> Let me hide myself in Thee;
> Let the water and the blood,
> From Thy wounded side which flowed
> Be of sin the double cure,
> Save from wrath and make me pure.
>
> Could my zeal no respite know,
> Could my tears forever flow,
> All for sin could not atone;
> Thou must save, and Thou alone.
> Nothing in my hand I bring,
> Simply to Thy cross I cling.

I programmed it myself one Sunday (over rock-band rhythm section, of course), just because.

Nowadays we see a lot of songs about fear. It's chic to psych ourselves up to attaining some kind of sense of bravery, almost as if it's really dangerous to get out of bed, go to work, and come back home again. The Savior Jesus is downplayed, because what's really important to me is that Jesus is the guy who relieves my fears. And He is, indeed, no doubt! But first and foremost Jesus is your Savior! And because you received his gift of salvation, the Holy Spirit dwells in you to empower you to "Be anxious for nothing!" What we sing about reveals what's in us. When we sing songs about our constant struggle to overcome fear, we reveal about ourselves the fact that we are not truly living in victory. A steady diet of these songs shows the world that instead of being powerhouses for Jesus like the characters of the New Testament, we're really just a bunch of wussies.

Then there's a whole batch of song lyrics (not to mention sermon content) that focus on what I can get from God. Let me just give you a little test. If you've been singing all morning about favor and seasons and seeds and blessings, and you find yourself at the end of the song set having never mentioned the cross or the blood, brother or sister you want to seriously reconsider what you're doing.

I don't want to get too persnickety about lyrics. There are so many ways to praise God and interact with God, and we need a variety of songs with a variety of messages to be able to communicate to God and about God effectively. I am just saying we need to be discerning about the words we choose to worship with. Here is the basic model we use at our church. In a given song service, we are typically going to touch these four themes:

1. Praising God for Who He is and what He has done
2. Reflecting on the cross, the blood, and the resurrection
3. Reaffirming of our total surrender to Him
4. Expressing a desire for relationship and revival

We aren't rigid with this model, but we give careful

consideration to what we're singing, and we do aim for balance.

Embracing the Cross

Jesus said, "If anyone desires to come after me, let him deny himself, and take up his cross daily, and follow me" (Luk 9:23). Taking up the cross means dying to self. It means putting our preferences to death. The idol of self is conquered when we take up our cross daily, and follow Him. The idol of self is inconsistent with the Christian life, because the Christian life is based on the principle of preferring others to self (Phl 2:3-4). The renewed mind is one that is completely fixated on God, and the "things above" (Col 3:2), and gives very little thought to my own issues in the here and now.

Let us consecrate ourselves, by the power of the Spirit, to embrace the cross, conquer the idol of self, and move forward with a renewed mind, worshipping the Lord in purity.

2
THE IDOL OF ENTERTAINMENT

This will surely seem obvious to some. As worship music has "progressed" into its current rock-band era, all of the rock-band traps have come with it. The sound, the look, the lighting, the show; all are things that can pull the focus away from God. This is what we might call **the idol of entertainment.** Many probably think we're actually getting better with this, given that the trend since the turn of the century has been away from the more "me-centered" Christian-artist model toward the more "God-centered" worship-leader model. But I'm afraid this shift simply makes the idol of entertainment less easy to pinpoint. Just because a musician on stage is leading a congregation in participatory worship doesn't mean he is not also performing, seeking attention, enjoying attention, gratifying himself through attention.

My heart is grieved as I see folks indicate their approval of certain singers, bands, and worship-leadership groups. The lack of discernment to realize that beyond the excellent music and smooth delivery these musicians carry zero anointing, it's discouraging. See, I don't care who you are or how many records you've sold. I only care if you are trusting the Lord with all your heart, representing the Lord well by all your actions on and off stage, glorifying the Lord with all your lyrics, and longing for the Lord to encounter you and the people you're ministering to, whether you get the credit or not. Many worship leaders (famous and not-famous) do have precisely these aims as their focus; many (famous and not-famous) do not.

Star Struck

I am blessed to work in an environment where we are consistently exposed to popular worship leaders, many of whom are wonderful people. But when they come around, it's obvious the young people are star struck. There's no doubt that these people get special treatment just because they are popular. Now, I believe we should show honor to whom honor is due. I believe we should treat our leaders well, particularly when they are our guests. And there are many godly men and women who are worthy of respect. That's not what I'm talking about. I'm talking about an unhealthy "default perspective" toward famous people that says that *because you are famous, I want to know you, I want to have some connection of relationship with you, because I hope that a networking connection with you will somehow lead to me making my break and becoming famous, too.*

The age of social media has really ramped up this unhealthy mindset. We live in a world driven by "likes" and "followers." Now more than ever, the average Joe can become famous overnight. And because that's now a

17

possibility, it drives our thinking, particularly among young people who haven't fully established or realized their identity. Even for those who have been trained that identity is found in Christ, the allure of the fame and supposed affirmation of social media is easy to succumb to.

So here we are, wanting to be famous, wanting to be liked, dying for affirmation from our friends and from the world. And we're not getting it. Because in the end, our friends and the world care about themselves more than us. And they're looking for the same affirmation we are.

True affirmation is only found in Daddy's lap. We may receive accolades from others, based on the things we do. But your Daddy (Abba Father) is the only One who gives you affirmation because He's the only One who truly knows who you are. He Fathered you. He made you in His image. When He looks at you He sees Himself, and He likes what He sees when He sees Himself in you. When you finally get a revelation of Who your Daddy is, the proclivity toward being star struck disappears. Because you realize that in Daddy's eyes, you're the star. That's affirmation.

The New Traditions

What are the real reasons we meet together as the Church? Every generation all the way back to the first century has had to parse through the differences between true biblical church functions and the traditions of man. Sometimes the traditions of man seem so benign, at first, that they can pass for dozens or even hundreds of years without being challenged. The abuses of the Roman Catholic church in the Medieval Era lasted more than a millennium! For more than 1000 years, there was no congregational worship, there was no worship in the language of the people, there was no

Scripture in the language of the people, there was no message of salvation by faith, and there was no understanding of the priesthood of the believer. The 16th-century reformers addressed these issues head on. By looking at what the Bible says, they were able to distill and separate biblical principles of worship from unbiblical traditions of men. And, broadly speaking, almost every denomination has, in its infancy, been birthed in a return to scriptural principles, leaving behind those who chose to stick with the traditions. Then, one by one, those denominations begin to lose the first love, lose the fire, lose the closeness to God, and become the next generation of tradition.

When they look back on us in 50 years, in 100 years, what will they say of the new traditions of the 21st-century evangelicals? Will they say that the 'Jesus People' of the 60's and 70's had it right, and the praise-and-worship era of the 80's and 90's were the glory days, and then our traditions began to crystalize in the 21st century? Will they long for the simplicity and authenticity of the Keith Greens, and wince at the spectacle of some of our modern worship groups? Will they mourn the loss of the choir? Will they bring it back in full force? Will they be more interested in hearing the voice of the congregation than in hearing the voice of the stars?

Calvin's reformation—for better or worse—included the removal of icons, the simplification of architecture, the devaluation of music. Was all of that taken too far? Probably. Was there good reason to react against the unholy elevation of human desires of that day? Absolutely. What are the human desires that have been elevated to an unholy throne in our day? Do dimmed lights really lead to better worship? Do fog machines help us encounter God? Is our volume level directly proportionate to our anointing level? Do our ripped jeans and flip-flops convey to God that we think humbly of ourselves, or do they simply show that we don't think highly enough of Him?

Many in the "contemporary" church believe that their "folk" music, "intimate" settings, and "informal" dress are all their way of being anti-tradition. But what we've failed to realize is, the Jesus Movement was 50 years ago. They may have been anti-tradition (and justified in it). But 50 years later, *we are the tradition*! And as we age, our children and grandchildren will be reacting to us. What will it be that we thought was so righteous, that they will be able to see as chaff?

I already see it happening in our youth. Many are seeing right through the show. They're embracing hymns, they're embracing the musical imperfections of true congregational worship, they're embracing stylistic diversity, they're embracing authentic worship, and they're not willing to abide the idols of the past two decades.

Back to my first question. What are the real reasons we meet together as the Church? To glorify God. To commune with one another, and with God. To hear the Word of God taught with integrity. We don't need a show to accomplish any of it.

3
THE IDOL OF STYLE

I'm a white guy, but my musical upbringing is not typical white-guy. I was raised Pentecostal/Charismatic. (I often joke that I'm half Pentecostal and half Charismatic, since my mom and dad were divorced during my teens, and many of those formative years were spent half at my dad's "Pentecostal" church and half at my mom's "Charismatic" church.) In both of those settings, in the early 90's, in Florida, our music was "praise and worship" music and Gospel music—a curious blend of Black Gospel and Southern Gospel, which both actually share a great many musical characteristics. We had choirs singing over "pop-band" rhythm sections. It was all keyboard-driven. I remember playing bass in youth band at my mom's church, and thinking the guitar player was weird because he was a rocker. He tried to educate me in the ways of rock; he was only slightly successful.

On the drive to church we listened to true Black Gospel on the radio, which I much preferred to the watered-down version we practiced in our sanctuary. To boot, my dad is a jazz lover. So from an early age I began to internalize those sounds, again very African-American. I played the saxophone in school, and I came to love the pop horn section sound of the great soul bands of the 70's such as Earth, Wind & Fire; Kool & the Gang; and Tower of Power. These sounds, of course, made it into our church music as well, though perhaps never as successfully.

This was, and still is, my style preference. It's who I am as a musician, primarily.

My first real exposure to what we now call Contemporary Worship Music wasn't until I met with a gathering of students in Columbus in 2004. Well, it shouldn't be surprising that I hated it. Guitars, guitars, guitars. Acoustic guitars, rock guitars. Not funky guitars! And rock-style singing, not soulful singing. And only four chords, oh! the famous four chords. This was boring music at its best. There was absolutely nothing for me to be interested in musically. (No offense intended if this is exactly the kind of music you like!)

And then I noticed something. The lyrics. For the first time in my life, I really began to pay attention to what I was singing. I realized that, because I hated the musical style, I was automatically tuning out the music and tuning into the words. I was beginning to conquer *the idol of style*.

Now fourteen years later, I don't know if I would say I have complete victory over the idol of style, but I'm pretty close. Sadly, I'm afraid most church members' stories are not as victorious. How many of us have adopted a "my way or the highway" approach to musical style in our churches! Just think back on the massive shift over the past 20-40 years. Many who came from a traditional background shrieked when the rockers invaded church music. And of course, the rockers weren't going to bend to the traditional crowd either. We began to have "blended" worship services, but for the most part, this was too blended for the traditional crowd, and not blended enough for the contemporary crowd. So we went to the "two services" model, not because we had too many people to seat, but because we needed to worship the idol of style. In the name of style preference, we adopted a model, unprecedented in the history of the church, that actually split the body of Christ in two!

And that, I'm afraid, was the better of the effects of the so-called *worship wars*. In many other churches, the contemporary crowd simply bullied the traditional crowd right out the door. Choir members were too amateur to be a part of the "professional" worship team, and many evangelicals felt that their only option was to leave their churches, often compromising their own doctrinal beliefs for a non-evangelical denomination where their musical style preferences were met.

Whole books have been written on this tragedy of the worship wars. And everyone agrees, it should not have been.

There's plenty of blame to go around. In broad strokes, the contemporary crowd should not have bullied the traditional crowd into submission, and the traditional crowd should have been willing to forego their preferences. But my intent here is not to paint in broad strokes. In fairness, I have no doubt that much of contemporary worship music was birthed in God, and many contemporary worship practitioners have advanced the style in a godly way. And I know that many in the traditional crowd did bend, did give way, did show their brothers preferential, deferential treatment.

No, what I am aiming at here is not a blame game on the global church level; I'm aiming at the individual. Specifically, you, the reader. What has been your experience with the idol of style? Have you recognized it and defeated it? Have you even bothered to notice that it's there? Is it holding you back?

The Apostle Paul tells us quite clearly how to deal with this idol. In writing to the Philippians, he exhorts:

> Let nothing be done through selfish ambition or conceit, but in lowliness of mind let each esteem others better than himself. Let each of you look out not only for his own interests, but also for the interests of others. Let this mind be in you which was also in Christ Jesus, who, being in the form of God, did not consider it robbery to be equal with God, but made Himself of no reputation, taking the form of a bondservant, and coming in the likeness of men. And being found in appearance as a man, He humbled Himself and became obedient, to the point of death, even the death of the cross.
>
> -Philippians 2:3-8

I don't believe there's anything wrong with having a style preference. Style is part of our individuality, it's how God made us, and how we have developed (Nature and Nurture). It would be extremely difficult for me to worship to Chinese music week in and week out. Chinese music does not resonate with my cultural understanding; I have no grid to be able to connect to it. We might as well just speak the lyrics. But if God were to plant me in a Chinese church, I would do everything I could to connect as best I could to have an authentic worship experience. I am not going to let musical style deter me from the point of the experience: to worship God.

You have no right to leave your church just because they

change the musical style. You have no right to choose a church based on musical style. You choose a church (and you choose to stay in a church) for one reason and one reason only, the Lord tells you what church you are to be a part of. If He says you should leave, then you should leave. Otherwise, you're there. And you're probably not there to "fix" the music either. Be faithful.

4
THE IDOL OF STRUCTURE

I was recently present for a Q&A session with the pastor and worship leader of a large church. Other worship leaders were able to ask these men about their philosophies and day-to-day operations. What leapt out to me was the importance placed on the structure of the weekly service, and consequently, the amount of time and effort devoted to the planning of the weekly service. By structure I mean that each element of the service was planned down to the most intricate of details. Each "segment" of the service was timed, down to a range of seconds. For this announcement, 1 ½ minutes, for that song, 2 ½ minutes, and so on. A lot of thought was given to how certain segments would be produced: perhaps a video to advertise such-and-such upcoming event, let's be sure to greet the visitors in a specific way, one guy in particular knows what to say and how to say it to make the flow in and out of that segment be appropriate. Clearly, much of this planning and structure was aimed at producing for the congregation, a *standardized routine* and a *consistent program* in which expectations for the meeting's structure are created, reinforced, and consistently met.

Broadly, we are speaking here of liturgy, which is not inherently a bad thing, and in fact exists in every church that I know of. By liturgy I mean the structural order of the congregational meeting. We generally associate the term liturgy with, for example, a Catholic Mass, but evangelical churches have their own liturgies. At the very least, we have music and a sermon. And many have much more structure than this, including such elements as offering time, communion, perhaps an altar call, closing prayer, etc. Structure and order in the congregational gathering are not wrong, but rather in fact scriptural:

> Let all things be done decently and in order.
> -1 Corinthians 14:40

So I am not denying the need for order. But I do believe that many churches have elevated this call to order so high that they are in fact worshipping **the idol of structure**.

Transitions and Flow

Among the current buzzwords in modern worship-leadership circles, two of the more prevalent are *transitions* and *flow*. Time and energy are put into sculpting transitions for the purpose of maintaining flow. As with most of the issues addressed in this book, neither transitions nor flow may necessarily be wrong on the surface, but when I hear these words, I have to wonder: What is the nature of the flow we're aiming for, and what is the real reason we feel we need transitions? My guess is, most of us are giving the wrong answer.

I think if we're honest, when we say we want flow, we're really saying we want a well-produced experience. Much in the same way one might produce a live show at a Florida amusement park, we want to keep the congregation engaged, we want to keep them focused, and we want to keep them coming back for more. Philosophically, we want our people to worship God; methodologically, we try to accomplish this by keeping them from being bored, distracted, and uncomfortable. To keep them from being bored, we offer a buffet of songs, styles, Scriptures, and exhortations, all in rapid-fire succession. To keep them from being distracted, we prepare and rehearse transitions—musical transitions, spoken transitions, logistical transitions—so as to avoid the "dead air" that we have somehow grown to perceive as worse than sour notes or false doctrine. To keep them from being uncomfortable we coach and choreograph our worship team members so that they don't look or sound "awkward."

This is not the kind of *flow* we should be aiming for. The flow that we should be concerned with acquiring and maintaining is the flow of the Spirit. Scripture indicates that we can quench the Spirit, and that we can grieve the Spirit. So everything we do, whether planned or otherwise, should be done with deference to the desires and actions of the Spirit of God working in our midst. Any transition that is planned with this aim is likely to be successful. Whether it's a Bible verse that exalts Jesus, a planned chord progression at the end of a song that allows for free expression of worship, or even a video clip, Spirit-led planning that has as its aim the ministry of the people to God, and the ministry of God to His people, will be pleasing to Him!

Some principles of transition are certainly worthy of consideration. For example, using Scripture or a biblically based exhortation to help the congregation see why we just sang the last song, or how it connects to the next song, or why it is important that we worship in the first place, can be very effective. But we must be on the lookout for an unhealthy philosophy that tends to accompany this methodical approach. We should not, as worship leaders, think ourselves to be God's cheerleaders. For any leaders who feel they must coax their congregations into worshipping week after week, who feel that without the leader there would be no participation from the congregation, I would submit that there's a much bigger and systemic problem that needs to be addressed. Your church does not need 30-second exhortations. It needs full-scale revival. *Anyone who needs to be given a reason to worship in order to worship is incapable of worship.* Nobody coaches me up on all the reasons I should love my wife, and all the ways I can express that love. If you love someone, it shows. If you love God, it shows. But most of the people in our churches don't even read their Bibles, they don't even give of their finances. Worship leader, if this sounds like your congregation, I would urge you to stop spending your time planning transitions, and join with your church leadership team to begin to plan a comprehensive approach to training your church in the foundations of the Christian life—starting with an impassioned presentation of the Gospel of Jesus Christ, which is not a call to a tidy little prayer of "acceptance" followed by a life of self-governed comfort, but is rather a call to a total life transformation marked by an utter fixation on and commitment to the desires of God.

The Early-Church Model

We don't know a great deal about what gatherings looked

like in the infancy of the church, but we know enough to know they didn't look like ours. First of all, they didn't really have music. This was not because they were against music, but because music, being loud, would have drawn attention to, and endangered, the persecuted church. What they had instead is given to us in Luke's history of the church:

> And they continued steadfastly in the apostles' doctrine and fellowship, in the breaking of bread, and in prayers.

> -Acts 2:42

Here is what the early church considered to be the essential ingredients of the church service. The apostles' doctrine, which nowadays we would call Scripture reading and sermon (remember the New Testament didn't exist yet), was a central part. So was fellowship. The early church practiced what was called the *agape* meal, or love feast, or what we now might call the fellowship dinner. You may remember Paul's rebuke to the Corinthians because they used these love feasts as license to get drunk and full while others who had less went hungry. Well that's how it isn't supposed to be done, but the fellowship of the saints is a vital function of church. Paired with these love feasts was the celebration of the Lord's Supper. Communion observance has always been an important part of the liturgical order of church, and it should continue to be. And finally, prayer. Certainly we have prayer in our church services, but it's often nothing more than a little tip of the cap to God. Many churches have prayer meetings, specific times set aside just for prayer. But these are the most poorly attended gatherings we have. No, friends, today's church service does not look much like the one in A.D. 40.

Another Revival Model

Contrast the prim and proper structure of the church described at the beginning of the chapter to Frank Bartleman's eyewitness account of the Azusa Street revival.

In the beginning in "Azusa" we had no musical instruments. In fact we felt no need of them. There was no place for them in our worship. All was spontaneous. We did not even sing from hymnbooks. All the old well known hymns were sung from memory, quickened by the Spirit of God. "The Comforter Has Come," was possibly the most sung. We sang it from fresh, powerful heart experience. Oh, how the power of God filled and thrilled us. Then the "blood" songs were very popular. "The life is in the blood." Sinai, Calvary, and Pentecost all had their rightful place in the "Azusa" work. But the "new song" was altogether different, not of human composition. It cannot be successfully counterfeited. The crow cannot imitate the dove. But they finally began to despise this "gift," when the human spirit asserted itself again. They drove it out by hymnbooks, and selected songs by leaders. It was like murdering the Spirit ...

No subjects or sermons were announced ahead of time ... All was spontaneous, ordered of the Spirit. ... We were delivered right there from ecclesiastical hierarchism and abuse. We wanted God. When we first reached the meeting we avoided as much as possible human contact and greeting. We wanted to meet God first. We got our head under some bench in the corner in prayer, and met men only in the Spirit, knowing them "after the flesh" no more. ... Someone would finally get up anointed for the message. All seemed to recognize this and gave way. It might be a child, a woman, or a man. It might be from the back seat, or from the front. It made no difference. We rejoiced that God was working. No one wished to show himself. We thought only of obeying God. In fact there was an atmosphere of God there that forbade anyone but a fool attempting to put himself forward without the real anointing.[2]

Ladies and gentlemen, I say to you I would rather have the power and manifest presence of God in that shack in Los Angeles than a 60-minute liturgical topiary with no Life, *any* time and *every* time.

Church leaders who worship the idol of structure don't bear sole responsibility for this epidemic. After all, they are simply giving the congregation what they want, aren't they? The American church has been lulled to sleep by the world. It is literally all around us, and we can't escape it. And the mass deception is that we have grown to believe that it's normal. From microwaves to pick-up grocery stores to high-speed internet, everything is fast, everything is available, and everything is dispensable. If I'm not happy with it, I can move on. And we want our church the same way. We want it produced, we want it packaged so as to be aesthetically pleasing, and we want it to be over so we can get back to the other 167 hours in our week where we do our own thing. Somehow this hour of "worship" satiates us and makes us think we are following God because we went to church and our neighbors didn't. It's all relative isn't it? Are you comparing yourself to the world and giving yourself a passing grade because you don't say as many curse words and don't look at as many dirty pictures? Are you telling yourself on the inside "I'm glad I'm not like one of them. I have my church, and at my church we get a sermon every week that tells us how we should live our lives, and I try to live that way, so I feel pretty good about where I stand?" Oh dear brother or sister let me tell you, you have strayed from the truth! My heart goes out to you, as does the heart of God, that you would read these words and repent and turn fully toward the Savior and run as fast as you can into His arms that He may show you His love and retrain you in His ways!

5
THE IDOL OF SPONTANEITY

I haven't seen much of the idol of structure at work in Pentecostal circles; I've seen just the opposite: ***the idol of spontaneity***. There's something that hangs around Pentecostal theology that says that if it's spontaneous, it's better, if it's spontaneous, it's God. Well, my Pentecostal friends, I've got news for you—it just ain't true!

Consider the history of worship. Let's start with the tabernacle, where God takes six chapters (Exo 25-30) to lay out all of the specifics of what to construct and how to construct it. Everything from the tent itself to the altar, to the laver, to the lampstand, to the table, to the incense, to the ark, to the priestly garments, and on and on. Think of all of the painstaking preparations that had to be made by the priests in order to carry out their duties. Do you think God would have accepted some man off the street spontaneously walking up to the altar with his spontaneous choice of animal? No sir! He had a prescription for acceptable worship. And it had to be followed.

How about the Davidic period. Did you know that during this era musicians were trained and apprenticed for five years before being admitted to the choir? And the Bible speaks of the musicians having direction, some under the direction of Asaph, some Jeduthun, some Heman (1Ch 25:1-7). Direction means planning.

From what we know about New Testament worship, it was fairly unstructured. But nowhere does the Bible record that a spontaneous act was deemed righteous solely on the grounds that it was spontaneous.

And what about today? No doubt most readers who attend a church that values spontaneity have seen the downside. The singer modulates a half step while the band stays in the original key. Or he tries to return to the chorus more times than planned, and the band is in the Bridge for four bars before they figure it out. Or Aunt Bertha comes forward to give her testimony and the pastor stands by with a nervous smile for 20 minutes trying to figure out how to gently shut her up and get his mic back. And let's not forget about our spontaneous prayers in which we heretically call the Holy Spirit "it," thank Jesus for sending His Son, and praise the Father for dying on the cross![3]

Inspired Worship

So am I saying we should not include spontaneous elements in our worship? Not at all. What I am saying is the fact that it's spontaneous is not what makes it of God. I would like to suggest that we exchange the word *spontaneous* for the word *inspired*. If it's inspired AND spontaneous, great; if it's inspired and planned, also great. What we want is for our worship to be inspired by God Himself! We want the

Holy Spirit to worship through us, leading us to a true and powerful encounter with God. Inspired worship can happen on Tuesday. I can't tell you how many times I have felt the Lord prompt a certain song or activity to be implemented on Sunday morning, seemingly at random, right in the middle of the week (and usually in the shower!). By taking the next 3 or 4 or 5 days to plan that into the worship service, it removes the spontaneity. But it's still inspired.

We may also have spontaneous, inspired moments "in real time" on Sundays, but I wonder if often many of these spontaneous moments could not have been executed just as easily and more excellently if we had only taken the time to listen earlier in the week. I am convinced God can speak just as clearly on Tuesday as He does on Sunday. Now, no doubt, there are times when He really does want to move spontaneously on Sunday, and He has His own purpose in all of that. But again, what makes that moment a God-moment is the fact that it was inspired, not the fact that it was spontaneous.

The Responsibilities of the Worship Planner

Here's a somewhat silly example to prove the point I've been making here. In what church, even in the most "free" of churches, would we allow a member to come forward right in the middle of a song, interrupt the song, and begin to make some sort of spontaneous exhortation to the congregation? Not many, if any. That's because it's out of order. The spontaneity of it does not lend any legitimacy to it. Even if the word is of God, the timing is not. In our church we allow for prophetic expression, from leadership and also from laity. But there is a protocol. And part of that protocol is the submission of an exhortation—both the word itself and the timing of that word—to leadership. Let everything be done in order.

We bring to each Sunday morning a plan. We usually have a prepared call to worship. We generally have a predetermined set of songs. We often prepare some transitional music or spoken word in between songs. We sometimes predetermine a period of free worship to follow a particular song. Sometimes we will specify a particular chord progression to sit underneath the free worship. Sometimes we'll just say, let's plan for the possibility of stretching this song out a bit at the end. We often program some ministry time, normally at the end of the last song.

That is our plan. We prepare the plan. We have rehearsals, and we try to make sure we all have a complete understanding of what the expectations are. Then 10:30 rolls around, and we lay the plan on the altar. We want God to have complete control over our service (indeed, over our whole lives!). If we believe God is prompting us to change a song, to call for ministry time early, to give an exhortation or a prophetic word (in between songs, at an appropriate time), to move into free worship at an unplanned time, or even to just stop everything and observe silence. If we believe we are hearing the voice of the Lord bringing *inspiration* to a moment, we yield. And yes, it's spontaneous. Some of these moments of inspiration, I'm convinced, could have been heard earlier in the week and planned, if we were listening better; others, I'm convinced, couldn't have been.

The responsibility of the worship planner is to plan, and then to put that plan on the altar. We are always to be yielding to the voice of God to do what He desires to do in our midst. If we hear Him early, and can work it into the plan, that's great. If we don't hear Him until we're in the moment, we still have to be willing to move with Him.

Part of what I am calling the idol of spontaneity is the idea that we can be derelict in our duties to seek the Lord and plan and rehearse what He wants to do, and then just be spontaneous on Sunday morning, and think that's ok. To attribute godliness to spontaneity, when it's really just unpreparedness. I heard a story recently about a pastor who basically played golf five days a week, and put no preparation into his sermon. Then he would wake up at 6:00 a.m. on Sunday and ask the Lord what He wanted him to say. Now my understanding is that God actually used this pastor to do His work on many occasions. But God was using him in spite of himself. It was not God's will and plan for the pastor to be lazy.

And there's a lesson there for us as well. We can't even assume that just because God uses a moment, that we were somehow justified in our lack of preparation. Sometimes God just does things in spite of us. We must be diligent to seek His face for what He desires to do. And then we must be willing to adjust the plan as we feel the Lord lead.

6

THE IDOL OF EMOTIONALISM

Another idol that Pentecostal/Charismatics have a reputation for worshipping is *the idol of emotionalism*. Both the idol of emotionalism and the idol of spontaneity are rooted in a mindset in the worshipper that the desire for the experience is greater than the desire for God. Now, I desire experiences. And I make no apologies for that. But experiencing God in a moment is never to be compared with walking with God for a lifetime. Winston Nunes used to say, "If you're slain in the Spirit, make sure when you get up, you walk upright." And we could add, "Run the aisles, roll on the floor, dance a jig, and cry your eyes out all you want, just make sure that when the emotion has subsided and you walk out the door, you walk upright."

An Old Problem

Christians have been struggling with the idol of emotionalism for almost the entire history of the church.

Notice how the giant of the early church, Augustine, confessed his guilt on the issue:

> In earlier days the pleasures of the ear enthralled me more persistently and held me under their spell, but You broke my bonds and set me free. Nowadays I do admittedly find some peaceful contentment in sounds to which Your words impart life and meaning, provided the words are sung sensitively by a tuneful voice; but the pleasure is not such as to hold me fast, for when I wish, I can get up and go. ...At times it seems to me that I am paying [these melodies] more honor than is their due, because I am aware that our minds are more deeply moved to devotion by those holy words when they are sung, and more ardently inflamed to piety, than would be the case without singing.
>
> ...All the same, I remember the tears I shed at the Church's song in the early days of my newly-recovered faith, and how even today I am moved not by the singing as such but by the substance of what is sung ...
>
> Thus I vacillate between the danger of sensuality and the undeniable benefits. Without pretending to give a definitive opinion, I am more inclined to approve the custom of singing in church, ...Nonetheless _when in my own case it happens that the singing has a more powerful effect on me than the sense of what is sung, I confess my sin and need of repentance._[4]

Now to make sure we have the proper perspective here, you must understand that Augustine is speaking of a time when church singing was unaccompanied by any musical instruments. Nor were there vocal harmonies. So here, writing about psalms and hymns sung in a single melody, with no lights, no fog, no amplification, no show, Augustine still recognizes the idol of emotionalism within himself. He confesses (in the underlined portion) that when he is more interested in the music than he is in the words, he has "sinned" and is in "need of repentance."

Church, we must war against the flesh, as Paul writes, recognizing its propensity to deceive us by calling those things good that are in fact evil. We must never mistake the emotional effect of our music for the salvific, restorative, Word of God that our music helps us connect with and proclaim.

Elevating the Experience

The reason that many people go to church today is to have an experience. I don't go to church to have an experience. I go to church to worship God. My primary aim in coming together with the congregation is to corporately worship the God who we've been individually worshipping all week. Along with worship, I go to church to fellowship with the saints, and I go to church to hear the preaching of the Word. I do not go to church to have an experience. I desire experiences, and I welcome experiences, and I am grateful for experiences when they come. But they are not the purpose of the meeting, they are fringe benefits of the meeting. We do go to church to receive, but what we are supposed to receive is equipping for the work of ministry, and this comes from our church leadership (Eph 4:11-13). We don't go to church primarily to receive some direct ethereal experience from God in worship. We go to church primarily to worship God, and to receive training in how to go out into the world and make Him known. If we have an awesome experience with God, that's wonderful. But if all we're after is the experience, and we aren't getting it, we will begin to get discouraged very quickly. And if we do have the experience … well, just because you had an experience doesn't necessarily mean you have had authentic worship. So, how might we judge our experiences?

The Test

Here is the test of your emotional church experience: Does it produce a change in your lifestyle? Do you walk away from that experience and begin to live differently on Monday, Tuesday, and Wednesday? Did your experience lead to greater levels of holiness, selflessness, and all-around Christlikeness? If not, I would argue your emotional church experience was worthless.

I'm not even saying it wasn't God. Many people experience God and yet walk away unchanged. Even the demons believe. The rich young ruler had a direct encounter with Jesus. He had a face-to-face conversation. And he walked away sorrowful. He walked away from his encounter unchanged.

A true encounter with God in worship is not like that. A true encounter produces lasting results. After Jacob struggled with the "man" in Genesis 32, he was left with a hip out of joint. He said, "I have seen God face to face," and he walked with a limp. His encounter with God produced a lasting effect.

When Isaiah saw the LORD high and lifted up with His train filling the temple, he didn't say, "Awesome! God is so good, and I love Him so much, and I'm so glad He's my buddy." He said "Woe is me! I am undone!" He was changed. And he walked away from that experience with a new posture: "Here am I. Send me" (Isa 6:1-8).

I love experiences. And I express emotion. But I have learned that emotional experiences are nothing compared to the contentment of consistent spiritual growth. We are called to bear fruit to God (Rom 7:4). Most of my spiritual experiences in church I've long since forgotten, but I can point to some fruit in my life right now. I've overcome areas of anger, lust, pride, control, impatience, and all-around immaturity. It's the fact that I can look back over my life and see how far God has brought me, see growth, see fruit. That's what brings increase to faith. Emotional experiences that are not coupled with a lifetime of progressive sanctification are really of no consequence.

7

THE IDOL OF PRODUCTION

Pentecostals are not the only ones who are subject to the idol of emotionalism. Our more reserved brothers and sisters simply manifest it in different ways. For example, they're much more likely to get their emotional high from *the idol of production*. Those who worship the idol of production treat the congregational gathering more like an evening at the theatre than a function of the body of Christ. Lights, cameras, action.

In my early days of ministry, I was privileged to serve in a large church with extensive resources, both in terms of finances and personnel. We had a large choir and full orchestra. We tended to put on several "programs" throughout the year, including Christmas and Easter and Independence Day. I enjoyed being a part of these productions, and to this day I don't have a problem with the idea of such an endeavor, in and of itself. But sometimes in this type of environment, there is more at work than just production, there is some idolatry. Consider, for example, a large church that might have a Christmas production budget upwards of a quarter-million dollars. Is that ok or is it out of bounds? One of the defenses given for this kind of spending is that there's nothing too good for the Lord. Which I certainly totally agree with. If a congregation feels that no price is too high for building projects, cosmetic upgrades, musical instruments, lighting, and even productions, I say go for it. We just have to be very careful that when we decide to spend money on "glitz," we really are doing it for the Lord's sake, and not for our own. And it can be very easy to confuse the two. If your church puts on the best Christmas production in town, does that bring more honor to God or to your church? If another church started putting on a better Christmas production, would you celebrate their success? Would you attend their production? Would you recommend their production to your friends instead of your own? Are we interested in getting the lost saved and giving the Lord glory, or are we interested in doing things that make us feel good about ourselves?

Another justification given for putting on large productions is that it's an evangelism tool, and people accept Christ at such events. It may be true that people get saved, but it is illogical to then conclude that those works of God somehow justify the event. For example, who's to say that just as many people couldn't get saved by doing a community outreach where hungry families are fed, underprivileged children get toys, neighborhoods get overhauled with basic repairs and paint jobs, etc? And you may say, well we could do both. And you certainly could. So, how do we know what to do? If certain decisions may be right in one context and wrong in another, how do we know whether we should do

45

them? Here's a little multiple-choice test:

1. Why do we do the things we do?
    a. We do the things we do for God's glory
    b. We do the things we do for our glory

2. What are the things that we decide to do?
    a. We do what God says
    b. We implement man's ideas

We can do the right things for the wrong reasons. So for example, we could receive direction from God to put on a Christmas production, or build a building, or whatever, and we could then approach that project with a prideful attitude. But we can also do the wrong things for the right reasons. We can put on a Christmas production, or build a new building, or whatever, with the right heart-posture of wanting to do something for God's glory, and yet He never gave us the instruction to go after it. The first question is a question of motives. The second is a question of direction. The first question is exponentially more important. God will not abide the heart of a man who is out for himself. He will either move on you to show you the error of your ways and break you into submission to His will and His purposes, or He will turn you over to your own depravity. The consequences for answering the second question wrong are less severe. Many in the church today don't even realize that God desires to speak and lead and give direction. They don't know that they can hear from Him in very practical matters. He isn't happy about this, but He seems content to let it be.

Of course, we can also do the wrong things for the wrong reasons, and the church has gotten itself in trouble here many times. But true power producing dynamic results will only come into effect when we do the right things for the right reasons. When we listen to the voice of God to give impetus to every project, every program, every sermon, every plan; AND we are faithful to carry out His desires in a posture that truly desires for the glory to go to Him and Him alone; we cannot fail! Pastors and worship leaders, if you can honestly answer *a* to both of these questions, you will see growth! It may not be immediate numerical growth, but your church will grow into the perfect will of God, and you will see fruit!

8
THE IDOL OF TRADITION

Most of our Sunday-worship experiences—regardless of denomination and style—have manmade traditions woven throughout. This is not necessarily a bad thing. Traditions, in and of themselves, are not evil, and are actually quite necessary. See, traditions are simply those things that we do that are neither explicitly prescribed nor explicitly forbidden by Scripture. There's nothing wrong with traditions. We probably couldn't survive without them. We have to have some amount of regularity and order to what we're doing. And since the New Testament is not terribly detailed in its description of what we should be doing and how we should be doing it, the door is left open for manmade traditions. As long as those traditions do not impede the work of the Lord, they simply become the regularly practiced methods of our Christian experience. But when we become so bogged down in our traditions that we lose sight of the purpose of the Father, the work of the Son, and the leading of the Spirit, then we begin to worship *the idol of tradition*.

What does the idol of tradition look like? It looks like the woman who is Presbyterian because her mother was Presbyterian, who was Presbyterian because her mother was Presbyterian, who was Presbyterian because her mother was Presbyterian. It looks like the man who becomes irritated when he enters the sanctuary to find that a guest is sitting in the seat he has occupied every Sunday for the last 42 years. It looks like the social event coordinator who throws a hissy fit when the pastor decides to forego the annual Christmas dinner. It looks like the board member who casts the lone dissenting vote on whether to accept the new worship leader because his vision included "new ideas."

The idol of tradition looks like the church that doesn't clap, doesn't shout, and doesn't allow hands to be raised. It looks like men in suits and ties who are not willing to get dirty to help somebody in need. It looks like praying to Mary. It looks like reciting the Nicene Creed from memory while daydreaming about next Saturday's fishing trip. It looks like a 60-minute ritual in which no lives are changed.

Why Ask Why?

The idol of tradition looks like a congregation full of people who have never stopped to ask why they do the things they do. Why do we sing the songs we sing? Why don't we sing the songs other people sing? Why do we raise our hands? Why don't we raise our hands? Why don't we have drums and guitars? Why don't we have an organ and a choir? Why don't the men in our congregation sing? Why do we do all of our songs in the same key Chris Tomlin does? Is there any correlation between the last two questions?

Why are we cessationists? Why do we baptize our

infants? Why don't we allow women to be part of our ministry team? Why do we give an altar call every Sunday? Why do we have 200 people on Sunday morning and only 34 people at Tuesday night prayer meeting? Why do we have small groups? Why do we have children's church? Why don't we ever get together with other churches to celebrate kingdom culture and learn from each other? Why don't we have any Black people in our church? Why don't we have any White people in our church? Why don't we ever see anyone get healed? Why don't we ever see anyone get saved? Why do the Pentecostals show up to the restaurant when we're leaving?

If you can answer all of these questions biblically, and feel confident in the direction God is leading you, great! If not, what is there that is worth rethinking? And if you've never even asked the questions, why are you just going through the motions? Jesus did not die so that you could perform a ritual 60-minute checklist each week! He died to empower you to change the world! WAKE UP, IDOL WORSHIPPER! And begin to worship God!

Worship in Spirit and Truth

Before Jesus gave His quotably famous doctrinal statement on worship in John 4:23, the woman he was responding to solicited his response from a most curious context. "Our fathers worshipped on this mountain, and you Jews say that in Jerusalem is the place where one ought to worship" (Jhn 4:20). Jesus' response was that it was no longer necessary that worship occur in either of those locations. In other words, Jesus came to eradicate all of the traditions that were unnecessary. The only thing left that was necessary, after Jesus' finished work was accomplished, was to worship in spirit and truth. The *how* of worship is not in traditions, but in spirit and truth. See, you cannot worship the idol of tradition if you are worshipping the Father *in spirit*, because traditions are born in the soul. They're not necessarily bad, they're just not spiritual. We can adhere to traditions all we want, but the moment we get so tied to those things that we cannot worship Him in spirit, we cannot move with Him where He desires to go, those traditions have become idols that keep us from true worship. Worship from your spirit, by the Spirit, is always fresh. Just like I can't successfully relate to my wife in a rigid format consisting of 60-minute scheduled meetings, written out communications, and a total lack of expressiveness; I can't successfully worship God that way either.

Similarly, you cannot worship the idol of tradition if you are worshipping the Father *in truth*, because truth is absolute, and traditions never are. Traditions are manmade. They come from our desire for routine; and sometimes they just come from a place of wrong thinking, or just plain silliness. Any time and every time truth challenges a tradition, the tradition must be discarded in favor of the truth.

Laying Aside the Commandment of God

That was Jesus' response to the Pharisees when they questioned Him about their traditions.

> Now when they saw some of His disciples eat bread with defiled, that is, unwashed hands, they found fault. For the Pharisees and all the Jews do not eat unless they wash their hands in a special way, holding the tradition of the elders. … Then the Pharisees and scribes asked Him, "Why do Your disciples not walk according to the tradition of the elders, but eat bread with unwashed hands?" He answered and said to them, "Well did Isaiah prophesy of you hypocrites, as it is written: 'This people

honors Me with their lips, But their heart is far from Me. And in vain they worship Me, Teaching as doctrines the commandments of men.' For laying aside the commandment of God, you hold the tradition of men—the washing of pitchers and cups, and many other such things you do." He said to them, *"All too well you reject the commandment of God, that you may keep your tradition."*

-Mark 7:2-9

Ladies and gentlemen, weigh carefully, as an individual and as a church, what are the things you do that are merely tradition and what are the things you do that are biblically mandated? Ask the Lord if any of your traditions are getting in His way. Ask Him if you are holding onto anything He wants you to lay down. And respond in obedience. Let's not find ourselves, like the Pharisees, rejecting the commandment of God in order to keep our traditions.

9

THE IDOL OF FREEDOM

When we say *freedom* in today's church, it's usually meant in one of three different contexts. The first is a wonderful privilege, the second is an undeniable biblical truth, and the third, which is the idol context, is heresy. First, many in the church prefer to worship in an atmosphere where they feel the *freedom* to express themselves; this is the wonderful privilege. Second, many of these (as well as other less expressive worshippers) make much of the *freedom* we have in Christ, which includes freedom from the guilt of sin; this is the undeniable biblical truth. Third, many of these hold a perversely inflated sense of *freedom*, which they think gives them license to operate outside of the biblical standards of holy Christian living; this is heresy.

What Freedom Isn't

A growing number of people in our churches today fall into this last camp. They talk about the finished work of

Christ, and they live as if their goal is to appropriate that work as much as possible. Immorality of every ilk is running rampant, from the pew to the pulpit. Pornography has reached pandemic proportion. Pastors are committing adultery. I've even heard of churches where the leadership dabbles in wife-swapping and the worship team bumps lines of cocaine right before the downbeat.

All the while they eagerly enter the sanctuary each Sunday morning ready to worship God, grateful for the freedom He has provided them. Freedom from every sin, past, present, and future. God vomits.

"Have I not clearly expressed My view on the matter?" He asks. "Is it not written in My Word, the one you own five translations of? Why should I say it again? Look and see for yourself."

> Now the works of the flesh are evident, which are: adultery, fornication, uncleanness, lewdness, idolatry, sorcery, hatred, contentions, jealousies, outbursts of wrath, selfish ambitions, dissensions, heresies, envy, murders, drunkenness, revelries, and the like: of which I tell you beforehand, just as I also told you in time past, that those who practice such things will not inherit the kingdom of God.
>
> -Galatians 5:19-21

> … Whoever does not practice righteousness is not of God …
>
> -1 John 3:10

> … Shall we continue in sin that grace may abound? Certainly not! How shall we who died to sin live any longer in it?
>
> -Romans 6:1-2

For if we sin willfully after we have received the

knowledge of the truth, there no longer remains a sacrifice for sins, but a certain fearful expectation of judgment, and fiery indignation which will devour the adversaries. Anyone who has rejected Moses' law dies without mercy on the testimony of two or three witnesses. Of how much worse punishment, do you suppose, will he be thought worthy who has trampled the Son of God underfoot, counted the blood of the covenant by which he was sanctified a common thing, and <u>insulted the Spirit of grace?</u> For we know Him who said, "Vengeance is Mine, I will repay," says the Lord. And again, "The LORD will judge His people." It is a fearful thing to fall into the hands of the living God.

-Hebrews 10:26-31

Friend, if I'm talking to you, listen to the words of the Lord. You're not experiencing the grace of the Spirit, you're insulting the Spirit of grace. Repent! There is no such thing as the worship of God in a life that is saturated in vile, habitual sin. You may think you're worshipping God. Think again, you're worshipping *the idol of freedom*.

A Reformation of Holiness

I believe a new reformation is on the horizon, and the hallmark of this reformation will be holiness. Once a central teaching in Christian doctrine, holiness was hijacked in the middle of the last century, and corrupted into legalism. For many, holiness no longer meant living a life free from sin, but rather living according to a set of rules about jewelry, hair length, skirt length, and make-up.

That's when the church began to rebel against holiness. But it wasn't really holiness she was rebelling against, it was the corrupted form, legalism. And as is typical of humanity, we swung the pendulum all the way in the other direction, claiming that grace was not just forgiveness and justification, but also a *carte blanche* to live any way we wanted. (Most won't say it that way, but they live it that way.)

There's no other way to put it: this is deception on a massive scale. The entirety of Scripture clearly and consistently indicates a mandate for holy living. "Be holy, for I am holy" (1Pe 1:16). It's never been optional, and it isn't optional for the 21st-century Christian. If the rich young ruler went away grieved because he couldn't give up his riches, do you honestly think the Lord will have any more tolerance for you if you can't give up your porn habit, or your mistress, or your habitual anger and lack of self-control, or your unwillingness to forgive? Yes, "If we confess our sins, He is faithful and righteous to forgive us our sins and to cleanse us from all unrighteousness" (1Jo 1:9), but confession implies repentance. We lay those things down by the power of the Spirit when we are reconciled to God.

The idol of freedom says that because I walked down an aisle one night and said a little prayer, I don't ever have to give another thought to my eternal destination. It's based on what Tozer calls the "accept-Christ heresy," the idea that I merely "make a decision" rather than "surrender my life." It's a concept of freedom that directly contradicts the Master-slave relationship articulated in the phrase "Jesus is Lord." I tell you there is no such freedom granted by a holy God. You simply cannot be your own master, and worship Him acceptably.

10
THE IDOL OF MUSICIANSHIP

A couple of years ago, I was put in contact with a pastor who needed a substitute worship leader for a Sunday morning. As we spoke on the phone, it became clear right off the bat that there would be some hurdles to overcome. He kept talking about how his church was on TV, and how it was critical that whatever they put in front of the public for consumption be professional and excellent. Since he didn't know me, he was giving me a good going over to see if I was good enough to meet his requirements. Now, some of that is ok. I certainly don't fault him for wanting to represent God to the world with excellence. But then he said this: "The number one thing I'm looking for in a worship leader is that he's got to be able to sing really well; number two is that he's able to lead worship." I politely turned down the opportunity.

Many churches today are much more concerned with the quality of their music than they are with the quality of their worship. This is very simply an act of disobedience against the

Word of God, which says "Set your minds on things above, not on things on the earth" (Col 3:2). Every time our mindset is unbalanced toward the things of the world over the things of the Spirit, we are in error. It is absolutely right and proper that we approach our church music with excellence, but our music should never be the primary focus of our lives or our ministries. When it is, we are guilty of worshipping ***the idol of musicianship***.

Excellence Without Idolatry

Our music should be excellent. It should be our best. "Play skillfully," the Psalmist exhorts in Psalm 33:3. Chenaniah was chosen to be the leader of David's tabernacle musicians because he was skillful (1Ch 15:22). But, as others have noted, he was not only skillful, he was first a Levite. In other words, his spiritual credential preceded his musical credential. This is what the pastor referred to above got backward. We must never put musical ability ahead of the ability to lead worship in spirit and truth.

Holiness Over Musicianship

There's been plenty of debate over whether we should allow unbelievers to be a part of our music ministry teams. Some view that as an outreach tool. Some will allow it for instrumentalists, but not for singers. Some will not allow unbelievers on the platform at all. I'll go a step further than this. According to Romans 12:1, living a life of holiness *is worship* (NIV, CSB, ESV). That means, not only will I not allow unbelievers onto our worship team, I have no issue with sitting-down believers who are not walking out holiness in their daily lives. We have "benched" some of our very best musicians for a season, in order to help them grow into a place of maturity and holiness from which they can return and minister successfully. Some may call that legalism. I call it good stewardship of the worship ministry. At our church, the leaders of worship will be the leaders of holiness.

11
THE IDOL OF DOCTRINE

I'm a doctrine guy. I believe it's really important to read and study the Word of God to learn as much as we can about who God is and what He expects from us. Anything that can be learned from Scripture, I believe we should be diligent to learn it. And live it. Nevertheless, there are some in the church today who are so enamored with doctrine that it actually stunts their spiritual growth. By elevating knowledge-about-God above God Himself, they worship **the idol of doctrine**.

True Christianity

One way the idol of doctrine manifests is through those who maintain the skewed view that Christianity is about *beliefs*. Faith, yes; beliefs, no. Beliefs have very little to do with the Christian experience. *Beliefs* implies *beliefs about*. The Christian does not merely hold a set of beliefs about God. He *believes in* God. As Martyn Lloyd-Jones once said, "It is possible for a man to give an intellectual assent to the propositions of the Scripture and still not be a Christian. Christianity is not at all concerned with our assent; it is very concerned about our true deliverance from sin." *Believing in* is another way of saying *trust*. And trust can only be secured through fellowship.

Beliefs about God are the things that result in denominations. They are all the little things that divide us. Where we *believe in* God, where we know Him as He truly is, we are united; where we have *beliefs about* God, we are divided.

The teen who has accepted a set of beliefs about God can be talked out of those beliefs by a "logical" professor. By contrast, no amount of logic or "facts" could ever convince me that my dad wasn't actually my dad. I know him.

Lyrics

Another one of the most common ways the idol of doctrine manifests is in the worship leader's approach to song lyrics. Now, I am very careful to choose songs for congregational worship that are theologically sound. I have been known to alter a word, or a line, or even cut an entire song, if I really don't believe it's biblical. However, the doctrinal content of the songs I choose for congregational worship is not what I consider to be the most important aspect of my ministry. Not even close.

I have seen so many students who begin to take an interest in theology, and as they grow in knowledge about God, they become obsessed with 'right' lyrics. They begin to turn up their noses at shallow lyrics. They really just become downright snobs. They excuse the behavior as "good stewardship" when really it's just an unholy desire to be right. But we're not called to be right, we're called to *look at Him*! Our righteousness is a gift of God, not something that we reason out. Friend, if I'm talking to you, if you're a theology snob, I admonish you to repent right now!

I once had a conversation with a teacher of the Word that I trust. As a developing teacher in search of guidance, I was explaining to him my concern over teaching what is right. "I don't want to be a heretic," I said. He reassured me backhandedly, "Well, let me stop you right there. You're already a heretic." I knew what he meant, and it did relieve the pressure. I am quite sure that when we get to heaven, each and every one of us will find out we were wrong about something. Half of us will be wrong about "eternal security" (once-saved-always-saved versus salvation-forfeiture) many will be wrong on the question of cessationism; many will be wrong on eschatology. I know where I land on these things, but I may be wrong. I do my best to read and interpret Scripture with integrity, and I trust God with the rest. I am much more concerned with pursuing fellowship with God than I am with pursuing right doctrine. And I am much more concerned with leading the congregation into fellowship with God than I am with presenting to them five perfect texts to sing.

Criteria for Lyrical Analysis

So, to recap, we need to be mindful of the lyrics we sing in church, without stretching this healthy caution into a stifling dogma. Let's go through the process of how we might accomplish this. And let's start with the initial phase of analyzing the lyric. I would suggest that a lyric may be critiqued in any of six ways. A song may be challenged on the grounds that it is: 1) false, 2) peripheral, 3) indirect, 4) shallow, 5) vague, or 6) clumsy. The first four criteria relate to the content of the lyric, whereas the last two relate to the song's craftsmanship.

A lyric that is false is not doctrinally correct. These songs are pretty tough to find. Most songs that one might think are potentially false are actually peripheral, indirect, or vague. A false lyric actually contradicts Scripture in every sense it can be imagined, and is therefore heretical. For example, a lyric that describes Jesus as "created from dust" is false. Jesus was not created from dust! Only one man was created from dust, and that was Adam. Eve was created from a rib, and all the rest of us were reproduced. But Jesus was not created at all! He is God Almighty, the Uncreated One!

A lyric that is peripheral is not biblically fundamental. This would include the prosperity-gospel repertoire, which is generally not so much false as it is unbalanced and distorted. Although peripheral songs are not explicitly forbidden, they should be approached with caution. It may be true that it's my season, or that God desires to bless me today, but if that's all I'm singing about, I am out of balance in my theology and my approach to worship.

A lyric that is indirect is not inherently Christian. That may sound worse than it is. We are referring here to songs whose lyrics must have some external Christian context applied to them in order to make them Christian. "Draw Me Close to You," by Kelly Carpenter, is an oft-cited example of this characteristic. If not for the capital letter, the "You" in the song could just as easily refer to a boyfriend as to God. Although many cringe at indirect songs, the fact is, we are singing these songs in church, and that alone provides the context that the One we're singing about is God. And some of the messages of these songs, such as expressing a desire to be close to God, and declaring that He's all we want, are very powerful themes for a song of worship. I would contend that many indirect songs are absolutely appropriate for use in congregational worship.

A lyric that is shallow is not theologically rich. Although the word *shallow* may sound negative, this category of songs is not inherently bad at all. It simply refers to songs that generally portray a single theme or concept, tend to be more repetitive, and do not provide much detail about who God is or what He has done (theological depth). I happen to love shallow songs, in combination with deep songs, and I program them all the time. In fact, I would say a song almost needs to be shallow in order to provide the worshipper enough time and repetition to meditate on God and our desire for Him. "Set a Fire" by Will Reagan, "Let it Rain," by Michael Farren, and "The More I Seek You," by Zach Neese, are just three examples of simple, devotional songs, much like the heart-cries of David in the Psalms, which are totally appropriate for congregational worship. Shallow is not bad, it's just different in its function.

A lyric that is vague is not linguistically clear. This could be a simple ambiguity in word choice or a more complex issue that leaves the listener asking "What does that mean?" Consider these lines by Edward Mote, for example:

In every high and stormy gale
My Anchor holds within the veil

See, modern worship songs are not the only ones with room for improvement. This line from the otherwise wonderful old hymn makes no sense. If we're at sea, what is a veil doing there? And if we're talking about the temple veil, why the seafaring metaphor? It's vague.

A lyric that is clumsy is not aesthetically pleasing. Some lyrics are either hard to articulate or awkward in the way the syllables are accented. Consequently they can be distracting, shifting the focus off of worship and on to the clumsiness of the lyric. Even the best lyricists can be clumsy at times. I've often wondered why "And Can it Be" starts with an *and*, when nothing came before it. The only thing I can figure is Charles Wesley just needed an extra syllable.

Now, just because we can critique a lyric in these ways, does not, in my book, mean we should immediately remove such songs from consideration of usage. I will never put a *false* song in front of my congregation. But I am willing to leave the door open for a peripheral, indirect, shallow, vague, or clumsy song. Those who worship the idol of doctrine would immediately dismiss most or all of these songs, constantly searching for "the best songs" to put before the congregation. But the best songs are not always "the best songs." Because there is another, ultimate test.

The Real Test

Once we have made it past the initial analysis of a song based on its lyrical content and craftsmanship, the true test begins. Does it work in our congregation? Here we apply two more criteria. Is the song *engaging* to the congregation? And is the song *effective* in activating the presence and ministry of the Holy Spirit? (When I say *activate* I simply mean that we want God to be active in our midst. I prefer this phrasing to the typically-Pentecostal "inviting" God's presence, because: (1) God is already present, and (2) the story of Christianity is that *God invites us* in to *His* presence!)

A song may be a perfectly fine song, and still fall flat. It may be doctrinally sound, it may speak to a central tenet of the faith, it may be inherently Christian, it may contain deep theological truths, it may be clear in its wording, it may be well-crafted. And yet it may, for whatever reason, neither engage a particular congregation nor activate God's presence. On the other hand, there are all kinds of imperfect songs that, engage the congregation and activate God's presence. These are the best songs, even if they're not the "best songs."

If the congregation is not engaged, if there is no sense that God is moved by it, if there is no greater revelation of His presence, if there are no bodies healed, if there are no spirits soothed (or convicted!), if there are no lives changed, the song may be "perfect," and yet ineffective. But if the congregation is engaged, and God is moving in the midst, I don't care how flawed the song is, as long as it's not false, you've got a keeper!

I can't tell you how many songs I don't particularly care for, that I nevertheless continue to program because our congregation engages with them in true worship, and God moves when we sing them. That is what it means to overcome the idol of doctrine. Should we be mindful of the words we put on our congregants' lips? Absolutely. But any worship planner who revels in pompously tossing out every imperfect lyric, thinking himself to be a general know-it-all and the supreme authority for all things theological, while he does not take into consideration that God may very well desire to use an imperfect lyric to bring revival to His people, worships the idol of doctrine.

12
THE IDOL OF RELEVANCE

The age of technology has brought with it many unintended consequences. In the past, what uniformity there was in our song selection, style choices, and worship methods, developed based on denomination (theological grounds) or geography (proximal grounds). So, for example, Presbyterian hymnals carried more texts with a Calvinist bent, and Methodist hymnals carried more texts with an Arminian bent. Appalachian church music would differ stylistically from that of the east coast cities. And so on. But now, since we are able to see and hear what's happening in churches across the globe, in real time, we have begun to develop a new form of homogeneity in our music and worship styles, and in our song choices. While this is not necessarily a bad thing, it does lead many to seek to "keep up with the Joneses." We see what is popular. We see what works for this church or for that parachurch movement, and we copy it, never stopping to think whether those songs are what God desires for our own congregation. We look out for the next album release of this or that group, and when it comes, we're the first to begin to program the latest "fad." And if you do any music from more than five years ago, you're out of touch. Again, I'm not knocking what any particular church or worship band/artist is doing. What I am saying is, each church is unique, and it is made of unique individuals, and we all have our little part to play, and we are all uniquely functioning members of the same Body. I am convinced that God does not want us all singing the same songs every Sunday. He wants to hear a special song from each church, from each individual. He wants to hear the Song of the Lord rise up to His ears. And He wants to move in each church, according to the needs of that church; He wants to move in each individual heart, according to the needs of that individual heart. But many of us are not interested in allowing our own voices—individual voices and corporate voices—to be heard. We're more interested in sounding like this or that popular group, because we think that if we copy success, we will achieve success. We think that if we look and sound like a particular ideal, we will draw the crowd that is attracted to that ideal. And we very well may. But drawing a crowd is not what we're called to do. And when we try to draw the crowd at the expense of trying to follow where He leads, when we care more about choosing the most popular songs than we do about choosing the most felicitous songs, then we are guilty of worshipping **the idol of relevance**.

13
THE IDOL OF COMMUNITY

Let's return to this question of why we "go to church." The church assembles to corporately worship God (through music, through giving, through partaking in the Lord's Supper, through baptism); to have fellowship with one another; to hear the Word of God preached; to pray together; and to be built up, and equipped for the work of ministry. Too many today elevate one or more of these functions so highly that they almost exclude the others. And that's where we begin to see problems. For example, you can't *only* come to receive the Word, and not also pour your heart out to God in musical worship. You can't *only* come to worship in song, and not also worship in financial giving. You can't *only* come to be built up and encouraged, and never give back through prayer.

One function that is elevated to a place of imbalance in the minds of many churchgoers today is fellowship. People are coming to church to make connections with other people, with no regard for their connection to God. *The church is not a social club.* We must make connections with fellow believers, but we must also make connection with God. You can't have one without the other. Jesus said "Love the Lord your God … and love your neighbor …" (Mat 22:37-39). John opened his first letter by explaining that he declares the Gospel message so "that you also may have fellowship with us; and truly our fellowship is with the Father and with His Son Jesus Christ" (1Jo 1:3). See, we cannot have authentic Christian fellowship with each other unless we are having authentic Christian fellowship with God. But that is where many in our churches today are stuck. They'll choose a church based on whether they have a strong youth group, or a thriving life-group program, or they just go wherever their friends go. For whatever reason, they feel the overwhelming need to cultivate personal relationships, but they do not feel the overwhelming need to cultivate their most important relationship. A person with such a mindset cannot offer acceptable worship to God, but instead worships **the idol of community**.

Small Groups

I have nothing against small groups *per se*. But from what I've seen, most of them are not accomplishing much. A lot of people love them. They love the cozy, informal environment. They love the opportunity to have conversations. They love the opportunity to be heard and valued. They love the tidy little devotional message. In many cases, they love the opportunity to tell everyone "what this passage means *to me*," as if it could mean something different to someone else.

If this is what pursuing God looks like for you, I have some devastating news. Chips and punch, a 10-minute sermonette, and conversations about sports, politics, and weather, do not a church make. Neither do they make a worshipper. You may be challenged by the Word, as the Word has a tendency to do, but you're not challenged by the people. Is small group the place where we all come together to pretend like our lives are awesome when we're really dying inside? Or are they the place where we can come and safely bear our souls with the hope and confidence of receiving support from family and ministry from God?

Men, where is the iron sharpening iron in your gatherings? Where is the call to holiness? Where is accountability? Ladies, what are you hoping to accomplish with your decorations and your tea and your shallow conversations about vaccinations and the latest car seat? What god do you serve? My wife, who has more disdain for these things than I do, calls it serving "the god of flowers." HA! Women, there's more for you! Spur each other on to be warrior princesses and kingdom powerhouses!

Small Groups with Purpose

I'm involved with small groups. But they don't meet every Tuesday night, and they weren't "organized" by "a person" in order to "meet a need" or "be relevant." My wife and I took another couple from our church to dinner this week. That's a small group. I went to lunch with two of my colleagues on the faculty last week. That's a small group. I have frequent conversations with my church leadership. That's a small group. These groups are in different levels of relationship-development. But they're all growing. And there are different levels of comfort to each. I can safely share different things with different people. But at every level, there is an opportunity for sharpening. An opportunity for me to speak into these peoples' lives to effect change. And an opportunity for them to speak into mine. There are men in my church who have permission to counsel me, and even correct me. And I them. These small groups, these relationships have grown organically. They're not forced, they're not awkward, they're not shallow, and they're not impotent. What they are is true Christian fellowship, just one component of a complete Christian life. Not idolized, but valued alongside other functions of the church, part of a lifestyle of worship.

I know that it's important in some cases to have organized small groups. Some folks have a hard time finding fellowship organically. And I know that many churches maintain very effective small group ministries, that aren't very much like the ones I described here at all. Let's just be sure that we are not worshipping the idol of community. Let's be sure that our fellowship with other believers is not the only function of the church that we're interested in. And let's be sure that we each have at least one core group of brothers (for men) or sisters (for women) that we can get real with, so that we can grow up into truly mature worshippers.

14
THE IDOL OF MINISTRY

So many pastors and worship leaders in the church today would not know what to do with themselves if they didn't have their positions. Many pastors are not willing to share their pulpits. They don't want outsiders. They don't want to allow the young men and women within their church who are called to ministry to have a training ground. And they definitely don't want to step aside for anyone who has a stronger gift, for fear the congregation will pine after "David who killed his tens of thousands." And then there are those who really do long to serve God, and they see God move in miraculous ways, and they get addicted to the "success" of ministry. Their lives often become imbalanced. They can lose their families, or even their morality, blinded by the trappings of God's work. Many worship leaders want the stage too, and they're not willing to share it either. They think that what they are doing is really important (and it is), and that it's important that they're the ones doing it (and it isn't). They don't trust that God can still move with someone else behind the mic. Or worse, if someone else led worship and God did move, that would invalidate them. Everyone I just described, on some level, worships **the idol of ministry**. The idol of ministry says that what I am doing for God is more important to me than God Himself. People who worship the idol of ministry get their "high" from being *used* by God rather than actually getting it directly *from* God. The idol of ministry manifests in various ways. Its worshippers may seek after it in order to fulfill one or more of these ungodly desires: control, power, fame, and gratification.

Control

The need for control is probably the most widespread manifestation of the idol of ministry. A pastor can be controlling, even among a tiny congregation of 15-20 people. There's something about ministry that lends itself to abuse through the spirit of control. We understand that in the church we must have clergy and laity. This is biblical. But any time we begin to make this distinction, we place control in the hands of the few (or the one). Even this need not be a problem as long as the leaders are able to continually walk in a posture of servant leadership, understanding that God is ultimately in control, and they are just the stewards of His will and direction for the congregation. This is very difficult to do, especially once you actually have the control. But it is something we must do. Guarding against the need, or even the desire, for control should be something at the forefront of every church leader's mind.

Control is the thing that says "I must have it my way." And it's difficult for a senior pastor, who essentially gets everything his way (or a board of elders that gets everything its way), to keep a clear distinction between what is "his way" and what is "God's way." As a man who "speaks on behalf of God," the senior pastor is in a quite delicate position of needing to constantly referee himself on this matter. And a senior pastor who is not submitted to a trusted covering, and even trusted laity, is in danger of failing on this point.

Control is the opposite of deference. As Christians we are called to be deferential. To prefer others to self. That doesn't mean we compromise core convictions, and it also doesn't mean that as leaders we allow ourselves to appease every opinion in the congregation. But it does mean we are willing to lay down our preferences on an issue if that issue is truly inconsequential to the biblical mandate of the church and the specific vision for our congregation. The color of the carpet, the design of the church logo, whether the building gets cleaned on Tuesday or Thursday—these are not issues that require the buck to stop with the pastor.

For the worship leader, control can look like any number of things, from musical style choice to decisions about the worship team participants. The new worship pastor who waltzes into the church looking to change everything to conform to his own image is likely worshipping the idol of ministry, manifested through control.

The worship leader does not need to have total pre-eminence over song selection. While we don't bend to the whims and desires of every church member, we can take into account the things that make our people happy. As the Lord leads, we can program Sister Lucille's favorite song or the Smiths' preferred musical style, as long as they fit contextually, even if they're not our favorites.

Power

The desire for power is certainly closely related to the desire for control, and can often be the next step in the sequence. It's also a bit more sinister. The main difference is this: whereas control says "I must have it my way," power says "through my control, I will influence you to give up something that will become a source of pleasure for me." We have seen the abuse of power for centuries in the church, from the indulgences of the Middle Ages to the cases of child sexual abuse of the recent decades.

The desire for power doesn't have to be as harmful as these atrocities. It could be as seemingly benign as a pastor who tries to work his way up to the upper levels of the denominational leadership. Or a worship pastor who pits himself against the youth pastor for first-place status in the senior pastor's eyes. Anytime the end game of what we do as ministers is "promoting me" rather than promoting kingdom, we are guilty of worshipping the idol of ministry, manifested through power.

Fame

Many today enter the ministry because they see it as a platform to notoriety. I think for most, there is a truly righteous desire to do the work of the Lord. But somewhere under the surface, there is something that says, "I want to do great things for God so that the world will say great things about me." The minister who is unable to kill the desire for fame is generally not honest with himself about his own heart and motives. He only hears himself say "I want to do great things for God," and never hears himself say "so that the world will say great things about me."

I see this idol often, with the young people I come in

contact with. You have a 21-year-old worship major who desires to do great things for God, and she's chomping at the bit to just complete her degree and get out into the church so she can begin to make a difference. Now it's time for an internship, and you set before this young lady two options, one small church that nobody knows, and one large church that has worldwide recognition. For that young lady, the assumption will be that the large church is the right move, that it's the God-move. There's no way the small church could be God's will. In her mind, the fact that there's an open door to a larger stage means that God must have opened it. And maybe He did, but maybe He didn't. It's equally likely that the enemy has offered a more attractive counterfeit, or that God is simply testing whether you will listen to Him or just assume.

God is more interested in our spiritual development than in our stardom. In fact He's not interested in our stardom at all. He allows some to become stars. Why? Some because He knows they can handle it. Some because he wants the song or the message to get out to the world, and He is willing to let the individual become famous—for better or worse—to accomplish His greater purpose. But just because He allows you to become famous should not be a reason to assume that your ministry and your life are pleasing to Him. There are simply too many counterexamples.

Gratification

This one is trickier to deal with because it actually begins with a wholesome and biblical desire, which is to enjoy being used of God. God really does want to use each and every one of us for His glory. He wants to do "greater things" through us than even the things Jesus did (Jhn 14:12). And He wants us to derive pleasure from the fact that He uses us to advance His kingdom on earth. The problem occurs when we begin to pursue that pleasure as an end unto itself, rather than pursuing God and enjoying the fringe benefits of that pursuit.

There are many in ministry who are addicted to the highs that come from seeing people saved, delivered from oppression, touched on an emotional level, and physically healed. Along with these highs come the lows of the normal, mundane life, which is unable to provide them the excitement of the divine manifestations. Because of the idol of ministry, these folks are not able to successfully carry out the true Christian walk, which entails a life of composure, stability, contentment, tranquility, and sobriety.

In addition, those who seek gratification through the idol of ministry can pay a heavy price, often experiencing the rejection of those they love most. Whole families can be lost when we pursue church ministry at the expense of our first ministry, ministry to our family.

The Pastor as Idol

For the congregation, the idol of ministry can manifest as the worship of the pastor. Church leaders with charismatic personalities and dynamic preaching styles can draw a crowd on talent alone. It may not even be any fault of the leader that he attracts many followers. He may be completely holy and anointed. But sometimes it's difficult for the immature believer (or even the unbeliever) to separate the preacher from the One he's preaching about. It's easy to begin to worship the big personality, and not even realize that we're no longer worshipping God.

Sometimes, of course, the pastor can add to this problem by encouraging the worship of himself. (This can be intentional or unintentional.) Nowadays we have church pastors who are running their own personal "ministries." The ministry of the church has been replaced by the ministry of the leader. This usually amounts to just preaching, though it could be more multifaceted. But God did not design his church to merely be a bunch of single leaders with dynamic insights and eloquent speech. He designed it to be a family in which everyone is valuable, everyone has a unique role to play, and everyone has ministry to do. Most of the ministry of the church is supposed to be happening outside the four walls of our meeting spaces. Laymen, you are the ones called to this ministry! Clergymen, you are the ones called to equip the laymen for the work of ministry. Pastor, if your vision for your church only amounts to you preaching to your people (or to the masses via media), and does not include the component of the people going out to do the real work of ministry in the world, you are not leading a New Testament church. Assess this carefully. It's too easy to say that our goal is to equip the people for the work of ministry, while in practice we're not even coming close.

EPILOGUE
A CASE STUDY IN SLAYING IDOLS

Today (as I write) happens to be the first Sunday that our church, All Peoples Church, is holding our Sunday worship service in combination with Court Street United Methodist Church. In a few hours, instead of leading worship in a contemporary setting, I'll be sitting in a pew with my family, listening to a pipe organ and observing the liturgy. I'd like to tell you the story of how that all came about.

All Peoples Church was established in Lynchburg by Pastor Bud Crawford eleven years ago. Three years ago, his son, Jeff, took over as leader. That was right about the time that my family started attending. In all of this time, we have been praying for revival. And we have believed that revival is on the way.

We have now seen things begin to happen. Two years ago we renovated our building to increase the seating from around 70 to 120, and since then it had been consistently about half full. Until one Sunday, when Jeff preached on the Azusa Street Revival, and three new large families—who all knew each other, but didn't know that the others were coming to our church that day—walked in the door. Since then, Sunday-morning attendance has doubled, in about six months. Several Sundays we have had standing room only. So when the lease on our building was set to expire, we had a decision to make.

As this deadline approached, Jeff believed that God was clearly telling him to take no action in trying to find a new building, and that He would "put it in his hand." When the time came to sign the lease, the Lord said "no." Fortunately, the landlord was gracious to extend an option for a 90-day lease, which we accepted. We are in that 90-day period as I write.

Meanwhile, the Lord has given us a vision for where we're headed as a church, and Jeff just laid out this vision in detail for us six weeks ago. We officially recognized a five-fold ministry leadership model (Apostle, Prophet, Evangelist, Shepherd, Teacher) for our church, and vision has been cast for where we are going, both geographically and spiritually.

But, no sooner than our long-term vision had been cast, our understanding of the short-term journey toward that vision would come into remarkable clarity. And the details have been unexpected, to say the least.

The week after the "vision" message, Jeff got a call from a man named Finny. Finny is a fiery fellow who runs the outreach in downtown Lynchburg called *The Lighthouse*. These folks minister to the poor and homeless, providing daily meals, clothes, and a space in which to rest and fellowship. The Lighthouse also has a community church, which is led by a retired Liberty University theology professor.

As Jeff was eating a bagel and minding his own business, the call came from Finny, "We have to meet." Jeff dropped what he was doing and went with Finny to see what he wanted to share. Finny drove him up to the doorstep of Court Street United Methodist Church, pointed, and said, "That's your new building." The building he was pointing to was built in 1901, it has dozens of rooms, five kitchens, and a sanctuary that seats 500 people!

The pastor of the Methodist church had reached out to Finny to offer his facility to The Lighthouse for them to use. Finny asked the Lord what to do with this building, and He told him to call five local pastors and tell them that they were all to come to Court Street and join together to make one congregation. Jeff was one of the five pastors Finny called.

I got the call from Jeff that night. At first, I didn't understand. I thought he was saying that five different churches would come and use the building at five different times. "No," he said, "the idea is that we all come together and become one." He then began to explain what that would mean. People are going to ask, "Who's in charge?" And some of the pastors and some of the worship leaders are going to want to be in charge. They will need to be in charge. We are going to have to approach this with the posture that we are willing to let anybody else who wants to "run the show" run it. Defer. "What about all the vision you just laid out?" I asked. "We have to be willing to lay our Isaac on the altar," came the reply.

At that point I became very excited, because I knew what was about to happen. God has given us a great vision, but He also knows that we have to trust Him with the realization of that vision, and not trust ourselves. He has asked us to lay our Isaac on the altar. To be willing to give everything up for the sake of encountering Him. He is saying to us, "Are you willing to experience what I have for you even if you're not in charge, even if nobody can point to it and say 'That was All Peoples Church,' even if you aren't the one leading worship when I reveal Myself to you, even if this person or that person or that other church name gets the credit?" Our answer is, unequivocally, yes!

The next morning I happened to be looking at the table of contents of this book. And it hit me. What does it look like to lay down all these idols in one stroke? It looks like Court Street United Methodist Church. We have to lay down the idol of self; we will not be able to make this new thing in our own image. We have to lay down the idol of style; we must be willing to hear and accept other musical styles. We have to lay down the idol of spontaneity; we will likely encounter much more structure. We have to lay down the idol of ministry; it's no longer All Peoples' ministry, it's officially God's ministry. If I never get to lead worship again, I'm willing to sit in the pew. We have to lay down the idol of doctrine; some of the leaders that were invited to join us lean to the Calvinist side, the Methodists obviously lean to the Arminian side, and many do not lean to the Pentecostal side. We have to be willing to hear things from the pulpit that we may not even agree with! Are we willing? Yes we are! Do we compromise our core convictions? No. But we defer all of our preferences, and even our stances on secondary doctrines, for the sake of seeing God move on His people, on ALL of His people.

Well, in the end, Jeff was the only one of the five leaders who agreed to come and be a part of this new thing. (That's not necessarily a knock on the other pastors. They had to move in the direction they felt God was leading, and that's not for me to judge.) As we began to have discussions with the other leaders (The Methodists and The Lighthouse), one other congregation jumped in as well. A group of young people calling themselves *Breakthrough Community*, mostly Liberty University students, with a 20-year-old pastor. This congregation has been praying for more seasoned saints to be able to walk with. And when this opportunity arose, they jumped at it.

So that's it, the Methodists, the Lighthouse, Breakthrough Community, and All Peoples Church. And today is the first Sunday that we're meeting together. Today, we are going to come sit in the pews, and the Methodists are going to "run church" the way they do it. Then next Sunday, they're going to sit in the pews, and we're going to "run church" the way we do it. Then we're all going to sit down together and figure out what to do next. Will it all work? Will it all stay together? We have no idea. But I can sense that God is in it. And I, for one, am willing to lay down my idols to see what He will do.

* * * * *

So, how about you? In reading this book, has the Lord revealed any idols that you are holding onto? Are you willing to lay them down? Are you ready to pursue more than just Christian business-as-usual? Are you ready to seek God more fervently? Are you willing to admit that there is more of Him to know? And are you willing to let go of all your pre-conceived notions in order to have an encounter? If it meant giving up more nights and weekends, would you do it? If it meant giving up your style preference, would you do it? If it meant merging with other churches, would you do it? If it meant giving up your own personal ministry, could you do it? If it meant hearing some secondary doctrines that you don't agree with, could you do it? If it meant giving up your choir in favor of a praise team, or giving up your drums and guitars in favor of a pipe organ, would you do it? Is there anything you wouldn't do in order to encounter God? Friend, I encourage you in the strongest possible way: don't stop slaying idols until your answer is *no*.

NOTES

[1] A.W. Tozer, *The Knowledge of the Holy* (New York: Harper Collins, 1961), 1.

[2] Frank Bartleman, *Azusa Street: An Eyewitness Account* (Gainesville, FL: Bridge Logos, 1980), 64-67.

[3] Praising the Father for dying on the cross is one of Paul Randlett's favorite classroom examples of what not to do as a worship leader.

[4] St. Augustine of Hippo, *The Confessions* (Book 10: XXXIII), trans. Maria Boulding, ed. David Vincent Meconi (San Francisco: Ignatius Press, 2012), 306-308.

ACKNOWLEDGEMENTS

Abba Father, thank You for calling me to write this book, and for revealing to me the thoughts You desired to communicate through it. It is written for You. Use it for Your glory.

My wife, Samantha, and our boys have given me the time and space to write, with no complaints. They are the best family a man could hope for. Thank you so much for supporting me through this project. Mom and Dad, thanks for giving me the foundations to be able to grow into an understanding of biblical worship. To Fred Guilbert, thank you for seeing in me what wasn't yet there, and for the constant encouragement in spite of what was. To Dennis Dunn and the wonderful folks at River Outreach Church, thank you for giving me the opportunity to grow as a worship leader. To Jeff, Bud, Adam, and my spiritual family at All Peoples Church, thank you for your trust, counsel, and support. Thanks also to APM for the opportunity to publish.

www.ingramcontent.com/pod-product-compliance
Lightning Source LLC
Chambersburg PA
CBHW060404050426
42449CB00009B/1902